My only one poem

One' you

Muhsina Kealamthodi

 pencil

ISBN 978-93-5667-200-0
© Muhsina Kealamthodi 2022
Published in India 2022 by Pencil

A brand of

One Point Six Technologies Pvt. Ltd.
123, Building J2, Shram Seva Premises,
Wadala Truck Terminal, Wadala (E)
Mumbai 400037, Maharashtra, INDIA
E connect@thepencilapp.com
W www.thepencilapp.com

Author biography

Muhsina Kealamthodi from Kerala she love write poems and stories novel.

CONTENTS

Very good

Dandelion root cause of my gallery
You full design your sent
I am in there
A magintic love
You unbelievable beauty
I am in your soul

Come back to me..

All in one

Night moon beautiful
Fantasy love
You give me

Red Rose circles around
Only you
Sun rise of the bloom enternal love
I drew your heart
For me
Only you breathing in my heart

Nice meet you

World soul you
I blindly darkness of my heart
You lighting unique way
I never forget
The night you sleep
I come to see you
You smile for me
You brightly coloured my life

Red Rose

Home that warm loveHome full my soulkeep waiting your
soul ..

In your eyes I see meThat's my homeYou are only magic
in my faceMake smileCupcake sweetMore Make YouOnly
one mineIt's time we meet againCome my wayYou live in
the earthI come for you all the wayWalking with youIt's
you..

Grape seed of my soulRarely FindI found youAll' around
the destiny of my heart
Red fully ocean skyI want to be the red stone of your soul
red rose of your smell

Remember

How could you so Amazing wonderful wow Define Love you growing fast that never endingIt's love you give meMore beautiful than Everything'sRunning eagerly towards youRaining session doesn't matter nothing effect me when I see you again in the every breath take my soul I alive only in your heart full love"

"You are my blue make every gray color beautiful garden rose make colour full ""Destiny created by the god give me your love fabulous passionate ""You are my beautiful angle peaceful song amazing rain warmest in all' the life ""Mirror Soul' you are glitter innovative brightly colored my life"" Very rarely Find you in the worldThat's Why without resion you are my angel""Fantasy in your attitude miracle in your smile wildly different imagination unbelievable beauty of perfume sprinkle of your soul""Casual and clarity glow in each day of calmness come to our own way magic light Fragrance of traveling miles I can smell feel you any place of in the world ""Nature silence mysterious way you throwing clean dot com here ""Only one poem on the earth nothing compared to you""Ocean wilderness step into the unimaginable happiness gentle eyes overflowing love a million times I looking for you legacy of excellenceShow you mirror deep wild fairy tale ocean in you ""Only you breathing destiny of my heart""Curving smile on your face wondering how you are trying to open the door already it's yourMagnetic you are my light house flower blooming with youGlory of the heaven it's all around in your heart beat speaking echo murmuring in my ears your name""That's magic wonder World soul you""Night moon calling you say nothing silence everywhere that found in the sky star written already in your eyes"

My only one poem

MY ONLY ONE POEM

The heart made moon
searching Longley soul'
That' belong one soul one heart
piece of different body
Always remember that piece of soul
When eyes cross soul to soul

" Give your love
I am very surprise to take Soulful Love "
"Brought me back to towards you
The mirror so beautiful with you
like glass of Moon"

"Heart touching love you made
it definitely come here"
"Galaxy flaying around in your eyes
Every time I love with you in my heart

enteral beauty touch with your eyes
smile on heart' reborn as a blue ocean diamond "

"How could you so Amazing
wonderful wow Define Love you growing fast
that never endingIt's love you give me
More beautiful than Everything's
Running eagerly towards you

"""

Angel hand

Sparkling light up my darkness of hidden treasure of
tremendous power of love""Milky mango testy remark on
the meeting is start time I see you""Night come more
beautifully because of you I love all the darkness faded
away glory of your Soulful love "

Make our own soul connect before

we borne infinity love it's always there for you

Time just fly with wings of fancy of your smell

Lighting unique bulb of vestibule of vagina monologuesMy
only mine your smile it is youLife is never be understood
because god written in you whole heaven in you for
meNice meet you again Soon Billion years after I reborn
again

Darling you more sweeter than

honey cream cheese softened butter melted chocolate chip
cookies milky white snow running with FantasyFlower in

My only one poem

the red rose gold smileFlowing through the skyI will show
you my dear love world

"Take one step closer than breath night

windows open come cent weather amazing starting
snowing here you warming soul bring me alive"You Vanlia
ice-cream with strawberry LoveMake find you well
respected all the best most of the heaven

You are the branches of my whole body still there is a
great gift
More I know more you made wondering how you are my
angelClimbing the mountain valley little more glassy flower
again missing your perfume around

Weather in your heart

Climbing the mountain valley little more glassy flower
again missing your perfume around the
weatherRemembering you

You made moon beautiful mirror see very clear close no
one found you are rarely Find in the earthGlad on me you
are only mineMagic around you win the story of our love
written by AllahMay coming to you something you can see
invisible eye'Red Rose in your heart gives youMelody night
you come from in the above lighting unique way my whole
heartWaiting for your time it's not word for word it's my
whole life

Beautiful soul you sleep well every time I looking at you
remember me capture the essence of the heaven youMeet
the world I meet you at your earliest time for very happy
moment come back home collect the keys for your heart
that is only mineTime day ago before again fill after out it
is sad happy boring interesting unknown but you are most
welcome precious gift my entire life changing whole
complete the form of a beautiful flower magic' fragrance
of youNight see I am going to be sleep wakeup dark scary
but you made starry night shining bird flying sky above
free from own soul

Feathers love you because you are own soul without featherless flying sky …. You are Angle Princes silence mysterious in your eyes only drop it wonderful moment I am going to be the world for heaven,….Living alieving in every minute precious because I found you

You look at the Sky thinking of meI know that it's you are my blue diamond Moonlight night shine on the earth

Night moon

Bright blue raining white drop brown soil melting all' in
your smile

Glimpse of Joy I found only in your eyes

Little more familiar that most honor you more than
anything else

I found without unknown on line unconditional eternal
Soulful beauty in your love

Bringing again back in the hole of darkness you spreading
Love lighting little bit more AmazingWay'Way'I never
imagine that it's youUnbelievable beauty in every where in
you there nothing without my life now

Centuries passed new year come and cross day changing as
a visit night sleep silence human living life they can't
remember fastly time' saying goodbye but in my Soulful
Heart remain in your fragrance soulAnd I always
remember you what time change you are always in meYou
are my entire eternity that I carrying everywhere with
meMy only one poemYou are mine most pretty love I
keeping come you back home where you belong to me..

Find answer of dream drew your heart blinking eyes of sea
rivers your own hand there is a me

Drew your life

You are highly teach me how much a human soul beautiful
but I found only in you

Magnetic soul always same as a blue violet in the earth
close to me

Find you all the sky aboveFilling with more
loveOverflowing unconditionalI find you in my heart

I never forget a moment that unknown attract more a
storyThat' only belong to me

All' the things far away but I am not sad I know you are
still there for meWaiting for me centuries

Most precious heaven gift

Living worthy of your smileI find you in my soul..

Walking in fantasy I imagine youWalking with you
foreverIn our reality..That's mi morning sweetness of wind
come back to you..

You bring back toward your way

Come back to me

I don't know that I follow everywhere you I think you my
dear angel

Flowing through the sky life fullLongley life only you
blooming blossom hill waiting for me

Wonder ..How you survive every wind in your life miracles
smile keep always without any complianceWow …. It's less
word Define your beauty make it wonderfulHide secret of
your smell most powerful weapon in the earth

That's only mine fantasy

Travel time change many thingsCome again your life
always stay there your heart only one poem

Living is worth itWhen you called meI am more alieving
every time..

Past written present invention future it's only you..

Come again my valley of red roseI still waiting for you..

Windows open long as a you come back homeHome made
with my heartHome that warm love

Rewrite

Me to get up you in my dreamsCome to your realityFuture definitely your red rose valley

Casual I take itBut it's you sincerelyMelting every your smileI want moreYou made palace of magic worldThe key your loveI am going to be a great gift for youIt's writing poem for youWritten destiny of Allah

You everywhere my every birth to a morning sound wakeup me with warm welcome

Fragrance Flame aliveOnly you come my home..

Give me your heartGive me your unconditional loveGive your every breathing soul infinity heavenYou are my angelThat' I found only in youGive me youI really your already when you don't know me you know me

Only one

Millions before and afterEternal our loveWithout speaking our wordsOur love story fragrance of our heartMake our love alive againThere is no stopContinue watching youMy life again living with youMy love..

Cristal bring a vibeMore fast I never familiarBut you must rewrite the skyI am going to happen to trueBecause it's you the reasonI love more than you love me

True TrueI totally wholly complete with you

Smile come when you smileI love when you smile because of meI want the goodness of God send to me really we mean to be togetherAlways forever eternal love

Turn your time

Time machine and I want use power for your happiness

How much I miss youSince before you bornI know you come again in the earthI am waiting for youWhen I don't where are you ?

All' the angle wings gotFlaying you with meI finally know thatYou where that is missing hereI only have one loveThat's you..

Morning belonging hereThat's why you are my unstoppableRare vastly castle Rock stone

Only bring a butterfly effectMostly high' colorful Liquid crystaleye-catching display invite your heart which is a good day

Marble building thousand yearsMemorable moments through shadow of your soulI am always protect your destiny murmuring slowly louder foot

I am know that

I know it's you

Every one happyBut I am happy when you come back to my homeThat's my heart beatRarely Find in you

Question serial numberI am only one answerMy only one poemIt's you belong to me

Your eyes speak thousand silenceI am only one secret you hide your heartButI can read your eyes without wordWho hide your heartI know the truthThat' still alive for meMy destiny loveYou always my only one poemI waiting ..Come our way home..Only you early rarely seenMy entire eternity keep your soul..

Enjoy your universe Fully loveStar's Longley MoonI see a magic shooting Star come

Fragrance

way through the sky looking at you remember the memory
whisper your name

Deeply down ocean lost my heartIn your ocean
eye'Bringing again bright blue diamond Moonlight
nightLike you like meI am really looking at only youThat's
Amazing wonderful wowLimit words cannot express how
grateful I am coming to my homeYou made billions of
years shooting Star in your eyes only one Moon your heart
that belonging to me

Rewrite the sky complete meBecause I so Longley
soulwithout youYou only bring my own way to towards
you I really want your loveOnly heaven Fully see in your
heart

Drawing freedom you loveI am the reason you comeBut
you are the reason my heart alive come back home

Under beautiful world only true your heart which is a great
gift

My solitary eagerly waiting for your Soul Sonorous Maid
my Soul

Mirror Soul'

Deep down a sprinkleRaise again phoenix birdSymbol of purity ringGive you your fingerOnly come from my soulful heart'AndYou are Soul' billion yearswaiting for my soul piceYou are my at comefrom above in the skyFor only for meWaiting minutes worthful for you..

Lilly flower soulRed Rose body of soulYour heart glassmirror diamond MoonMe the only your own

Spray all' the perfumeYou are special centMade with my heartI know you are mineIdentify without any eye'sBecause you are

Come fast

Time is you a beautiful Time"
Very excite me all' the timeVery nice surround in your
lifeVery good tell you morning magicAll' in you
Silence mysterious butyou more mysteryBut I love that
wayMore beautiful mystery
happiness sweet smile more wonderful in your face
Single night looking in the darkOnly your heartBright blue
lightFlowerSmilingLittle FantasyMore expensive priceless
moon
Write a letter meaning is youEach one character edgeMean
to me
Darling you mean to meThe earth create pointWe are
togetherWe are come together in the earthDifferent way
But you are meant toOnly mine..
Window open clearly see SkyAlways remember meWhen
sky always sameWherever goIt's sameIt's remember
youIt's same
See you again one moreSee you again every timeSee you
again living mirror in my eyes open heart for you
Quick world of your day is the time.I used to Longley in
the skyBut you call meI am happyBecause you I can live
hold your handI am still very happy I found youThe all'
Longley road you made blooming fragrance flowing your
way

To see you

Charm of youMore elegant design youSurprise when I found youYou made really happy

Holding your handIt's foreverI will flaying with youIn the skyYou are the reasonI am come in the earthYou are my only infinity heaven love

Everything is change because we meet a human soul spiritAlways connect centuriesIt's destiny to meet youAllah made our love soulfulOnly you are mineEvery time I see youMy heart leave the placeCome to your sensesI want you only youMy angel loveYou are my beautiful WaitingCome true soon..

Time to time turn to youSomething missingBut I found all' my piece of soul in your eyes only

Dream sewn together in river sideView of my whole lifeI am willing to follow everywhere you goMy birth to eternity you alwaysThe soul I love to see..

Sky open a door we can go together homeMy loveYou my dear love

Dam silence of in your eyesWorried meCalmness come from in your heartI heard you very distanceMade more valuable precious for you

Millions star passing in the galaxyMy eyes only one MoonIt's youI found you

My Kingdom of soulVery rarely seen blue diamond Moonlight

My heart

When you are my way to homeWhy you fear of timeBecauseI am only Waiting forYou come..Fragrance Flame alive in youI can feel the centdistance from the world

Time year's passed but my soul searching everywhere for you..

My lovely eye'sCan you come so fastI want see you againMore beautiful thanEverything's my life

When Rain come I will be there for you with umbrella

Turn your heart only for meI am missing youYou know thatYou are my angel

"World soul in to view need a heart of diamond eyes"

"Home made because I know you come"

Future unknown definitely undefined like the blue magic oceanDeeply secretive you going under more misery more WonderfulAnd I in your way ..

A lamp light in the colorless rainbowYou come lighting unique rainbowSorrows of pain' darkness of Summer looking at the skyMirror of moon come with colorfulRainbowYou are magnetic soulI never see in all the centuriesI passed my life

Quick jumping my thoughtI never want miss your smileAlready early come in your side

I never forget missing fragrance flavor you come filled with your love

Rainy rainy complete every drop rain blinking in the eyesHidden behind the scenes in my heartWalking towards you where you sandWith a umbrellaThat' is fully only for you
World see in your eyes meMean I am the world

Hidden behind every smile

You hidden treasure of the heaven

Silence mysterious hurtBut when you silent my heartBurning with unimaginableWhen you speakI am alive with you

Thousand miles walkmillion years passingSession of weather changeAll I do sanding for youmissing your perfume sprinkle eye's crossing the border of the heavenI never thought without youWalking in the any world I goLet be together forever ..Warm hand gestures during a beautiful flower magic' youI really want hold youMost precious heaven gift..

Allah is a control heaven and earthAllah is a great gift for you

Pray to you are my angelThat' only written my destinyLove fantasy Dream wakeupWith your armsMorning murmuring sound comeSoul return to backI only searching for you

Fragrance Flame aliveAlive with your loveSmile with unconditional loveYou are Magic wonder World..

You are someone who can make it wonderful moment I am going to be the world you are my beautiful garden angle

Darling you more than anything elseYou more gorgeousYou think aboutWith everywhere youInner soul waking all' the beauty of Invisible destinyOutermost you heaven light shineBlue diamondFully you rose fragranceI

am in youThat's my life..
"Mirror to mirror you to me"

Drewing

Drawing freedom you loveWriting a letteryou say most beautifulWaiting for when you comeI am drawing a door open for youOnly you..

You are a miracle happen to meBut no one know your valueOne they realize who you areMost precious heaven angle soulHappen in the world rarelyBut it's happen for me..Queen of the heavenyou will be in my heartKing of your soulI am in you..

Lucky gemstones are you still want us most of the heaven it's the door

My heart beat very happy lyrics written in your eyesonly drop it my eyes

A long time ago mountain viewKeep calm down to earth windowOpen your love view mineOpen the door for you..

Fragrances Red Rose valleyName of the heaven I see in you

"How rich your heartValuable precious priceless "

Earlier in the orange is smelling like dark night I see a shadow following me with orange smellNothing found myselfWithout parishion in the earthI only have one love youCome and save meIn the earthI want live with your smile

You are viewing mode which is a manipulate the world

Dandelions valley of the heavenDeeply in love with youCalmness name is butterfly eye'sCross your fingers crossed for me

Nice meet unimaginable happinessHidden treasure of the heavenFor you

Treat me whatever your mind answer of what is meaning of this is a good time to explore new ways of life with you

Made mine

You made aliveness the worldI see you in my heartA fabulous day come to meThrilling bright colour in my lifeYou are the branches blossom myLongley tried heart'I call you my angel

I hold everything in my handButYou are wonderful soulFree with everything ownYou keep wakeup meTo say very happy love

"Hold you in every breath soul "I never forget your smileThat' made my destiny loveI call you infinity heavenYou give me your heartI am happy to see you again

"Beautiful eyes sparkle her heart for me"

"Nature of the beauty come your fragrance soul of the heaven"

Red Rose fantasy perfumeShowering peace in your eyesOpen the door of the heavenLittle the world where you goThere is a good timeMost precious love

"Build the kingdom of Heart romance passionately speeding your love"Vanlia my Vanlia you again mineRaining with you foreverI will be there for your umbrellaCan you come with me my worldOnly made for youIt's you.. My Moon..

Distance between placeour soul oneWe are together foreverEvery life your and me

"Fragrance of you might be from me"

Wonderful love beautiful soulCome together with you forever

"flower fantasy world I am in your heart that Amazing dream in my reality "You are my fantasyYou are my imaginationYou are my reality

Come to Home

Come with me..

Really you are my angel true your life miracles of the heavenCome to my home only waiting for you in centuries passed always for you..

"My shadow of your soul mate with your heart"I look at you remember me capture your heart the way you don't knowFinally made a smile on your faceOnly one Moon your eyes only drop it wonderful dream come true

Dark very deeply going inside the boxYou com lighting unique rainbowI do have a million yearsBut you have a beautiful smileChange my darkness in bright lightColoring my lifeWith your colorFinally we meet againIn new centurySmile..

Know more about more you blink growth of the heaven"Lighting unique moon in the sky I think but that is only for meAgain we love in the skyWe meet again in the earthBeautiful butterfly ..

"Lovely dream lovely soul mirror of Soulful Heart"

Wind come with a message towards you miracle of love say I love youTouching magic' of feather in my destiny loveYou..You are crystalline limestoneInfluence my heartVery bright bewilder mysteryIt's you Occan of blue diamond scrawlMagic fantasy ocean Whirlwind create wow Invisible between our soulFully in your eyes..

Dancing in the love Therefore youOnly you Smile on your

faceThat' belong to meMy beautiful Moon
Drew your heart which is a good morning my beautiful garden angleKnock the door open for youOnly one poem

Smile come to the heaven

On the wayDraining the skyWithout your beautiful smileStar move towards moonI was wondering in the darkYou come fragrance My light

I running towards youLike non stop loveLike no one knowsYou are the reasonI come to alive

Midnight silence beauty of youMy heartRarely come to the earthShould I touch your soulI found youIn my whole heart waiting for youDandelion root in the chemical of the sweet smile mixingEvery corner of heart'Sunflower my darknessShining unconditionalOnly you made come to meIn the corner of my worldDarkness You are sunflower sunshine..

Thanks

Mirror Soul' enter your body
Fragrance of flowers blooming
Lilly Red Rose valley

Come to the world
Surround sound like calling
That' is our only live once again
We going to meet
Are you ready
But you can do that
Mine always forever

In to your fantasy

Living alieving

Destiny created our love
You made it definitely
I will never know that
You are my beautiful garden angle

Come to the sky
In my heart beat
I love the feeling
Only one poem
Draining my all energy only
For you
Beautiful soul

Every time

You are the best
You are my beautiful
You are my angel

Are you still there
For me
But I always waiting for you
In to your life
Dancing in the dream
With you beautiful place
I can't imagine
But only you

For you

Love with you
High' and low
You are my beautiful
Come again that' make sure
I will show you
My heart

That' is our only ringing call
Be mine
No one come to you

Queen

Vanlia you again for your sweet
Need for a while to get up
I gone crazy
I want you

Running eagerly towards you
Mine heart' reborn
Because you call me

www.ingramcontent.com/pod-product-compliance
Lightning Source LLC
LaVergne TN
LVHW091137180726
843490LV00008B/3042